WHEN HEAVEN DREW THE LINE

A Complete Spiritual Memoir

TAVACA DORSEY

Printed in the United States of America.

ISBN: 979-8-9939537-3-1

DEDICATION

To God — the One who called me, kept me, carried me, protected me, and taught me what no human could teach. You are my steady hand, my strong tower, my instructor, and my inheritance.

To my daughter — your love, your light, and your strength were often the voice I heard in the quiet moments when I wanted to give up. Everything God is building through me, He is also building for you.

To my family — thank you for your prayers, your support, and every moment of encouragement. Even in the places we do not yet understand, God is weaving purpose.

PURPOSE

This book exists for anyone who has ever walked into a moment they could not explain. For the ones who felt something shift in a room but had no words for it. For the ones who battled silently because the war was not physical — it was spiritual. For the ones who knew God was pulling them somewhere unfamiliar and still said yes.

My purpose is to give language to what was happening behind the scenes, to reveal the truth about unseen atmospheres, and to testify of the God who trains His warriors in wilderness places.

VISION STATEMENT

When Heaven Drew the Line is a complete spiritual memoir — a journey through spiritual obedience, unexpected assignments, divine training, and supernatural clarity.

This book captures how God called me from my living room in Atlanta into a desert battleground I did not see coming. It reveals how He sharpened my discernment, exposed hidden warfare, strengthened my identity, and prepared me for the higher terrain waiting on the other side.

The vision of this book is simple:

To awaken the ones who are called.

To strengthen the ones who are fighting.

To prepare the ones who are about to be activated.

ACKNOWLEDGEMENTS

I give all honor to God — for seeing me, choosing me, and training me in ways that stretched me beyond what I believed I could carry. Every chapter of this book is His hand at work.

To my daughter — you are my joy, my reminder, and my why. Thank you for loving me through every transition and cheering me forward even when you did not understand the full weight of the assignment.

To my family — your love has always been a covering.

To every reader — may this book open your eyes, strengthen your spirit, and remind you that you are never unprotected, never unseen, and never out of God's reach.

CONTENTS

PART I

THE ASSIGNMENT

CHAPTER 1 — THE CALL TO LEAVE

I wasn't planning to leave home.
Not the city I knew.
Not the life I had built.
And certainly not the comfort of everything familiar.

But God rarely asks permission when He is ready to move you.

For months before the assignment, I had been lying on my
sectional couch, watching sermons by Cindy Trimm and Jolynne
Whitaker. I didn't know it then, but God was preparing my spirit.
Jolynne stirred my prophetic sensitivity. Cindy sharpened my
authority. Little by little, God was conditioning my ears and
awakening gifts I didn't even know were inside me.

I was learning without knowing I was in class.

Then one ordinary day, in the quiet of my apartment, God
whispered something that pulled the ground from under me:

"It's time to go."

The words didn't come with details or explanations.
They came like instructions — firm, disruptive, and
unmistakably divine.

I didn't have a plan.
I didn't have a strategy.
I didn't even know where I was going.

But obedience hits different when God has already been training
your spirit in advance.

So I said yes.

And that yes became the doorway to a desert I didn't choose —
a battleground I didn't anticipate —
and a version of myself I didn't yet know existed.

CHAPTER 2 — OBEDIENCE IN THE UNKNOWN

Obedience sounds beautiful until it asks for something uncomfortable.

I didn't know the details of the assignment.
I didn't know the timeline.
I didn't know the challenges waiting for me in the desert.

All I knew was that God said go — and my spirit couldn't ignore it.

People think obedience comes with certainty, but it doesn't.
It comes with instruction, not information.

I remember standing in my living room, suitcase open, wondering why I felt such urgency. Why now? Why this? Why leave everything familiar for a place I had never seen?

I didn't get answers — I got peace.
And sometimes peace is the only confirmation God gives when the path requires faith, not understanding.

When I told my daughter, she didn't fight me.
She didn't try to hold me back.
She didn't try to talk me out of it.
She simply honored my decision, even though she knew it came with emotional weight.

She understood something many adults still struggle with:

When God calls you, no one else can answer for you.

As I packed my bags, I wasn't thinking about warfare, spiritual assignments, or divine training. I wasn't thinking about what was waiting behind the sand. I wasn't thinking about the environments God was getting ready to expose.

I was just moving with God.

Obedience became the bridge between who I was and who I was about to become.

I didn't know that a storm was waiting.
I didn't know the atmosphere I was stepping into would test everything God had placed inside me.
I didn't know that the journey would become a testimony.

All I knew was that obedience was the only way forward.

So I picked up my suitcase, took a deep breath, and stepped into the unknown —
not because I was fearless,
but because I was called.

CHAPTER 3 — SIGNS, SIGNALS & SPIRITUAL LANGUAGE

Some people learn through words.
Some through instruction.

But God trained me through atmosphere.

Before Kuwait ever became a battleground, God began teaching me the silent language of the spirit — the subtle shifts, the inner nudges, the quiet alerts most people overlook because they're waiting for something loud.

But the spirit world rarely speaks loudly.
It speaks through:

• pressure
• peace
• timing
• movement
• discernment
• invisible resistance
• sudden clarity
• inner alarms you can't explain

I didn't always recognize these signs. Not at first.

Sometimes God will train you long before He explains why.

Looking back, I can see that God had been preparing me for Kuwait long before my feet touched the desert. He trained me to feel when something was off, to sense when something was watching, to recognize when something was shifting around me even without a word being spoken.

Discernment wasn't something I learned in a church pew — it was something I learned by survival, by observation, by walking through environments that didn't match what they looked like on the surface.

Before Kuwait, the Holy Spirit had already been sharpening my senses, tuning my hearing, stretching my awareness.

I just didn't know what it was for.

But obedience will always lead you into the training ground for your calling.

God doesn't teach spiritual intelligence in safe places.
He teaches it in places where you actually need it.

Those late nights in my living room weren't random. Jolynne Whitaker and Cindy Trimm weren't just encouragement — they were preparation.

God was teaching me to:

• recognize witchcraft
• discern manipulation
• understand spiritual pressure
• read atmospheres
• pray without speaking
• hear Him beyond noise
• know what was demonic or divine

Those teachings didn't just inspire me — they trained me.
They awakened the prophet inside me.
They prepared me for a place where physical eyes weren't enough.

So when Kuwait came, even though my mind didn't understand, my spirit recognized the assignment instantly.

This chapter wasn't about fear or confusion — it was about **recognition**.

Recognition of calling.
Recognition of threat.
Recognition of spiritual activity.
Recognition of divine protection.

I wasn't walking into Kuwait —
I was walking into purpose.

CHAPTER 4 — THE FAREWELL & THE FAITH WALK

Leaving home is easy when you are excited.
Leaving home is different when you are being called.

When I packed my bags for Kuwait, I couldn't explain it — but I felt a deep stillness mixed with a quiet urgency. Not fear. Not anxiety. Something else. A pull. A knowing. A spiritual gravity that told me:

This is not a trip.
This is an assignment.

But I didn't yet understand the weight of that word.

Saying goodbye to my daughter was the hardest part.
She didn't try to stop me.
She didn't question me.
She simply said, "Mommy, just be safe."

There was maturity in her tone — like she sensed something spiritual pulling me forward.

Leaving my apartment — my sanctuary, my altar — felt like stepping out of a cocoon. Those walls had held years of prayers, warfare, revelations, and healing. That space had held God.

As I closed the door, it felt like He whispered:

"Now go. What I placed inside you must be activated outside your comfort zone."

Walking through the airport felt unreal. Everyone else was traveling; I was transitioning. I boarded the flight with peace that didn't make sense.

No fear.
No anxiety.
Just obedience.

This wasn't the end of a chapter —
this was the beginning of a calling.

And sometimes all God needs is a yes.

A yes with shaking hands.
A yes with teary eyes.
A yes that doesn't have all the answers.
A yes that trusts God with the unknown.

That yes changed everything.

CHAPTER 5 — THE SILENT TRAINING

When I landed in Kuwait, the first thing that spoke wasn't a person — it was the atmosphere.

People around me were laughing, talking, irritated, rushing. But spiritually, I felt something heavy, thick, charged — as if the air itself carried history.

This was my introduction to territorial pressure — the spiritual density of a place that reveals what operates there.

Before I met a single person,
before I saw the dorms,
before I understood the base,

the atmosphere greeted me first.

When I entered my room for the first time, the Holy Spirit settled gently — not loud, not dramatic, but sure. My room felt claimed. Covered. Shielded.

I didn't know it then, but God had already marked my space.

This season wasn't about learning rules or schedules — it was about learning people and spirits:

• who watched me
• who avoided me
• who felt threatened
• who felt drawn
• who reacted to my presence
• who shifted when I entered a room

Every silence was a signal.
Every interaction was a lesson.
Every strange moment was revelation.

God trains His warriors differently.
He trains them through awareness.

CHAPTER 6 — SENT WITH A SWORD

Before Kuwait became a battleground, God placed a sword in my spirit. Not a physical one — a spiritual one.

A sword of discernment.
A sword of authority.
A sword of awareness.
A sword of clarity.

Real warfare is not loud — it is strategic.
Sometimes the strongest attack is silence.
Sometimes the greatest defense is presence.

I didn't announce myself.
I didn't boast about my anointing.
I didn't try to prove anything.

I simply showed up.

And spiritual pressure revealed itself immediately.

Some people were drawn to me.
Some were comforted.
Some were curious.
Some were threatened — not by me, but by the light inside me.

When God sends you with a sword, your presence alone becomes warfare. You don't have to swing it.

The atmosphere recognizes it.

CHAPTER 7 — UNSEEN PROTECTION

God's protection often comes disguised.
Not always as angels with wings, but as:

- closed doors
- delayed conversations
- sudden unease
- blocked paths
- quiet warnings
- inner discomfort

From the moment I arrived, I felt watched — not by people, but by heaven.

Walking through hallways, something followed me — but it was covering.
In the DFAC, I felt observed — but it wasn't danger, it was protection.
Outside in the desert air, I felt presence — not fear, but assurance.

God whispered through every moment:

"You are not alone here."

Every time manipulation tried to approach me, God blocked it.
Every time evil tried to disguise itself, God exposed it.
Every time danger tried to come near, God cut it off.

When God assigns you to a battleground, He also assigns angels to your defense.

You are never unprotected.

Reflection & Integration

Part I: The Assignment

These questions are designed to help you pause, reflect, and integrate what you have read. Take your time. There are no right or wrong answers — only your honest response to what is being stirred within you.

1. What did you notice in yourself as you read about the call to leave? Did anything stir, resist, or resonate?

2. Have you ever experienced a moment when God asked you to move before giving you the full picture? How did you respond?

3. Obedience often requires stepping into the unknown. What would it look like for you to say yes to something you do not yet fully understand?

4. In what areas of your life are you sensing spiritual instruction but waiting for more information before you move?

5. What does it mean to you to be trained by God in advance — before you know what the training is for?

6. How do you recognize when God is preparing you for something, even if you cannot yet see what it is?

7. Reflect on a time when you felt spiritual protection or unseen covering. What did that experience teach you about trust?

PART II

THE AWAKENING

CHAPTER 8 — THE DESERT DETAIL SHIFT

Some assignments are physical and spiritual at the same time.
The desert detail was both.

Each morning, the sand met the sun like a warning and a
promise. The air felt alive — still, silent, but spiritually active.

In the desert, everything unnecessary is stripped away.
You can't hide behind noise.
Atmospheres become louder.
Motives become clearer.
People become more visible.

The desert became my classroom of discernment:

• who changed when I walked up
• who watched me from a distance
• who grew irritated
• who grew curious
• who grew intimidated

Patterns formed quickly.
Movements revealed motives.
Timing revealed truth.

Kuwait wasn't just a location — it was a testing ground.

My spiritual senses sharpened with every shift of the wind.
With every step in the sand.
With every interaction or silence.

The desert was showing me:

Your spirit speaks before your mouth ever does.

CHAPTER 9 — THE SLOW UNRAVELING OF TIME

There are seasons when time stretches — not naturally, but spiritually.

Everything slows down because God wants you to see what you would normally miss.

Conversations carried hidden meanings.
Glances revealed motives.
Pauses revealed intentions.
Avoidance revealed truth.

People who once moved freely around me began moving differently. The atmosphere reacted to my obedience, and God opened my eyes to see:

• motive behind a smile
• strategy behind silence
• truth behind hesitation
• warning behind energy shifts

Nothing was random.
Everything was revelation.

God whispered:

"You're not imagining it — you're discerning it."

CHAPTER 10 — HIS PRESENCE IN THE QUIET

There is an empty quiet.
And then there is a full quiet.

In Kuwait, the quiet was full — filled with God's presence.

He met me:

• on the walk to the post
• in the stillness before sunrise
• in the desert wind
• in the heaviness or lightness of a room

The quiet became my teacher.

God reminded me daily:

"I go before you.
I go with you.
I stand behind you."

His presence made the wilderness bearable and the assignment clear.

I wasn't alone.
I was accompanied.

CHAPTER 11 — ACTIVATED BEFORE SUNRISE

One morning, before dawn — the fourth watch — I woke up with fire in my spirit.

Not fear.
Not adrenaline.
Activation.

God whispered:

"Get up. Now."

I moved with precision I couldn't explain.
I prayed with authority I'd never felt before.
Heaven was summoning me.

Then came the corridor walk.

It wasn't emotional.
It wasn't dramatic.
It wasn't planned.

It was obedience.

Something in the dorms had been operating spiritually — watching, manipulating, pressing. But when I walked that corridor, heaven walked it with me.

The air shifted.
The atmosphere broke.
The territory was reclaimed.

God didn't send me to start a fight.
He sent me to end one.

CHAPTER 12 — THE DAY OF FIRE

If Chapter 11 was activation,
Chapter 12 was confirmation.

God's fire showed up — not flames, but spiritual heat and justice.

Suddenly:

- masks slipped
- alliances fractured
- manipulations collapsed
- motives were exposed
- darkness became confused
- monitoring lost its power

God said:

"This far — no further."

Pressure lifted.
Control shattered.
Opposition dissolved.

Not because of me — but because of God.

He had drawn a line in the spirit.

CHAPTER 13 — ANOINTED FOR THE UNKNOWN

This chapter was about realization.

Realizing how protected I was.
Realizing how awakened I had become.
Realizing how deeply God had developed my discernment.
Realizing my spiritual identity carried weight.

This was the moment I stopped shrinking.

I embraced:

• my sensitivity
• my discernment
• my authority
• my spiritual identity
• my calling

I didn't feel ready —
but God said I already was.

The unknown wasn't scary anymore.

I was anointed for it.

CHAPTER 14 — WHEN HEAVEN DREW THE LINE

This wasn't the end —
this was the turning point.

Heaven declared:

"This far — no further."

Spiritual interference collapsed.
False power structures fell.
Dark alliances scattered.
Atmospheric control broke.
Everything that stood against me bowed to God.

The assignment in Kuwait was complete.
Heaven reclaimed the territory.
God shifted me into elevation.

When heaven draws a line,
everything aligns.

ABOUT THE AUTHOR

Tavaca Dorsey is a spiritually awakened believer, called and activated through real-world battlefields, divine assignments, and supernatural training grounds. Through her experiences in unseen atmospheres and spiritual warfare, she brings clarity, authority, and language to spiritual realities many feel but cannot articulate.

Her mission is simple:
to strengthen the called, awaken the sensitive, and guide believers through the hidden dimensions of their purpose with boldness, insight, and the leading of the Holy Spirit.

NOTES

Reflection & Integration

Part II: The Awakening

This section represents deepening awareness — the awakening to what is really happening beneath the surface. Use these prompts to explore what has been awakened in you.

1. What spiritual realities became visible to you in this section that you had not seen before?

2. Have you ever walked into an environment where the atmosphere felt off, even though nothing was visibly wrong? What did you sense?

3. How do you discern the difference between your own anxiety and a genuine spiritual alert?

4. When have you experienced pressure that was not about you, but about what you carried or represented?

5. What does spiritual precision mean to you? In what areas of your life is God asking for greater intentionality?

6. Reflect on a season when you were being tested. What was God refining in you through that experience?

7. What does it mean to complete an assignment without needing emotional closure or external validation?

PART III

THE LINE IS DRAWN

Author's Note

This section was not written from the middle of a battle. It was written after the dust had settled, the noise had faded, and clarity had taken its place. This is not a continuation of conflict, nor is it an explanation of what came before. It is a record of what becomes visible when pressure lifts and perspective changes.

This section is for those who have endured seasons that required strength, discernment, and restraint — and who now find themselves standing somewhere quieter, steadier, and more spacious than before.

You do not need to know the details of what happened to recognize what is happening now.

This is not retreat.

This is elevation.

Chapter 1 — The Work Was Finished

Chapter 15 — The Work Was Finished

There was no announcement when it ended.

No moment where everything stopped at once. No visible marker that said, *this is the end*. What I experienced instead was a quiet certainty—the kind that settles in the body before it ever reaches language.

I knew the work was finished because the resistance was gone.

Not subdued. Not silenced. Simply absent.

What I had been sent into no longer required my presence. Not because I forced an ending, and not because I stayed long enough

to see vindication or resolution with my own eyes, but because the assignment itself had completed its purpose.

This is something you only recognize after you've lived through prolonged pressure. When you've spent enough time discerning atmospheres, navigating systems, and remaining steady under conditions that were not designed for your flourishing, you learn the difference between endurance and completion.

Endurance feels tight.
Completion feels clear.

I did not dismantle anything. I did not expose anything. I did not need to confront what had once resisted me. What could not continue simply stopped standing.

That distinction matters.

There are moments when God calls you to engage—to speak, to awithout inviting you into the aftermath. This was the latter.

The work concluded without requiring my commentary.

There was no need to look for evidence or confirmation. The absence of tension was the confirmation. The lack of obstruction was the answer.

When the assignment ended, nothing followed me forward.

No unresolved pull.
No lingering obligation.
No unfinished emotional business demanding closure.

The clarity was internal before it was circumstantial.

I understood then that not every victory looks like confrontation. Some victories look like release. Some endings come not with noise, but with permission—permission to move on without explanation, without defense, and without revisiting the terrain that once demanded your strength.

This was not retreat.

It was completion.

And once I recognized that the work was finished, movement became natural. There was no urgency in leaving, no need to dramatize departure. I did not have to convince myself it was time. I did not have to talk myself into obedience.

The door was simply no longer there.

When Heaven draws a line, it does not require you to stand guard over it. The boundary holds on its own.

The work was finished—and I was free to move forward without carrying the weight of what no longer existed.

Chapter 16 — Leaving Without Looking Back

Leaving did not feel like escape.

That surprised me.

I had imagined that departure—whenever it came—would feel dramatic, emotional, or heavy. That there would be a sense of finality so strong it would demand reflection or explanation. Instead, what I experienced was something quieter and far more telling.

Release.

There was no urgency attached to my movement. No inner pressure pushing me out the door. No fear of consequence chasing me forward. I wasn't running from anything, and I wasn't bracing for what might follow.

I was simply clear.

That clarity mattered more than the movement itself. Because when you leave a place prematurely, part of you remains behind—watching, wondering, replaying. But when you leave after completion, the attachment has already loosened before your body ever changes location.

I did not need to convince myself it was time.
I did not need to rehearse what had happened.
I did not need to resolve every question in order to move on.

The absence of resistance was the signal.

There is a difference between choosing not to look back and having no reason to look back. I experienced the latter. Nothing in me reached backward for validation, explanation, or emotional closure. The place I was leaving no longer held authority over my direction.

That was new.

For a long time, my attention had been trained on vigilance—watching patterns, monitoring shifts, staying alert. When you live like that long enough, stillness can feel unfamiliar. Movement without tension can feel almost suspicious.

But this was not numbness.
This was discernment.

I understood then that when God finishes a work, He does not require you to linger to make sense of it. He does not ask you to stand in the aftermath proving that the ending was justified. Completion does not need witnesses.

It simply releases you.

I left without narrating the moment to myself. Without marking it as significant. Without turning it into a scene that needed interpretation. I did not carry a running commentary of what I was leaving behind.

That, too, was part of the healing.

Freedom does not require surveillance.

When God removes you from a terrain, He does not expect you to keep watch over it. The work of holding the line is not yours once you've crossed it.

I did not look back because my vision had already shifted forward.

∧

Chapter 17 — When the Noise Finally Stops

At first, the quiet felt unfamiliar.

I didn't notice it all at once. Silence arrived gradually, almost cautiously, as if my system needed time to trust that it was real. After living for so long in a state of alertness, stillness didn't immediately register as peace.

For a long time, noise had been constant—not just external sound, but internal pressure. The subtle hum of vigilance. The mental scanning. The awareness that something could shift at any moment.

When the noise stopped, my first instinct was not relief.

It was curiosity.

I began to notice small changes. My thoughts slowed down. My breathing deepened. I could sit in silence without feeling the need to fill it.

That's when I realized how loud survival mode had been.

The absence of noise revealed how much energy had been spent just staying ready.

As the quiet settled in, clarity rose without effort. I didn't have to strain to hear God. There was space.

Peace revealed itself not as absence, but as order.

Silence rearranged priorities. It separated what was necessary from what was merely loud.

The noise stopped—and clarity took root.

Chapter 18 — Perspective Changes Everything

Perspective does not arrive all at once. It settles in gradually, shaped by distance and stillness.

From higher ground, details arrange themselves.

What once felt personal revealed itself as positional. What once felt chaotic revealed order. Distance did not erase what happened—it clarified it.

I could see patterns instead of personalities. Systems instead of moments. Purpose instead of reaction.

Perspective restored proportion.

What once consumed my attention no longer occupied my horizon.

Seeing clearly was not about more information.
It was about the right distance.

C

Authority is unhurried.

Urgency dissolved as confidence settled in. I no longer felt compelled to explain, defend, or rush outcomes.

Judah goes first not because it is loud, but because it is positioned.

Authority does not negotiate its existence.

Movement came when it was time. Speech came when it was necessary. Action followed clarity, not pressure.

This was leadership from higher ground—quiet, deliberate, and effective.

Chapter 20 — Remembering Without Pain

Memory changed its tone.

I could remember without reliving.

Experiences moved from injury into understanding. Memory became instruction, not interruption.

Healing did not erase the past—it repositioned it.

From higher ground, memory became a witness, not a wound.

Chapter 21 — Higher Ground Requires Less Explanation

Elevation simplifies communication.

I no longer felt obligated to translate my decisions or justify my distance.

Clarity replaced conversation. Boundaries became quieter, but stronger.

Explanation is not always a bridge. Sometimes it is a tether.

Higher ground teaches restraint.

Chapter 22 — The Terrain Has Changed

I am no longer where I once stood.

The line has already been drawn. The work has already been completed.

This is not the unseen realm yet.
This is the climb that prepares you for it.

I stand on higher ground—steady, clear, and unencumbered.

Closing Reflection

Higher ground is not earned through striving.
It is entered through obedience.

When the work is finished, silence follows.
When the noise fades, vision sharpens.
When perspective changes, authority settles.

You do not need to return to what God has already closed.

Stand where you are now.
The terrain has changed.

About the Author

The author writes from lived experiences shaped by faith, discernment, and obedience through seasons of pressure and transition. Her work centers on spiritual clarity, inner authority, and the journey from endurance to elevation.

Reflection & Integration

Part III: The Line Is Drawn

This section represents clarity, completion, and elevation. Heaven has drawn the line — not out of rejection, but out of protection and purpose. Reflect on where boundaries, clarity, and higher ground are emerging in your own life.

1. What becomes visible when the noise finally stops? What clarity is waiting for you in the quiet?

2. Have you ever experienced completion without closure? What did that teach you about God's timing and your own need for resolution?

3. What does it mean to leave something behind without looking back? What are you being called to release?

4. Reflect on a boundary that God has drawn in your life. How has that boundary protected you or redirected your path?

5. What does higher ground look like for you right now? What perspective shift is taking place?

6. How do you distinguish between authority that is rooted in urgency versus authority that is rooted in clarity and rest?

7. What line is Heaven drawing in your life right now — and are you willing to honor it?